MY PRAYER BOX

A Gift To God

MY PRAYER BOX

A Gift To God

Obtaining Perfect Peace through Prayer, His Gift to Us

Mike & Lynn,
God bless you all
with His perfect peace,
love, strength & especially
His joy. You are in
my prayer box →
Mary Ann

MARY ANN HASLETT

Prov. 3:5-6

To order additional copies of this book, contact:
Xlibris Corporation
1-888-795-4274
www.Xlibris.com
Orders@Xlibris.com
20162

CONTENTS

Acknowledgements 7

Dedication 9

Preface 11

1—The Gift of Prayer 13

2—Childhood Prayers 17

3—God's Word on Prayer 23

4—Intercessory Prayer 33

5—Family Prayer 39

6—Walking with God in Prayer 43

7—My Prayer Chair 47

8—Answered Prayers and Blessings from God 51

9—Why Pray? 61

10—Your Prayers 65

Journal Pages 69

Scriptural References by Chapter 123

Acknowledgements

First and foremost, I thank our Lord God, for inspiring me with the ideas and words to write this little volume, and for directing my path as I embarked on this project. From start to finish, He lovingly provided me with guidance and placed many angels along my path to help me complete it. I am so thankful for those "angels":

For my wonderful husband, who encouraged me and helped to proof read my work, all my love and thanks.

For Dr. Leslie Holmes, who was the first to review my manuscript, he encouraged me to have my work published. When I asked him to pray for me, he would pray right on the spot. On one such occasion, he called me to see how I was recovering from my surgery. I know his prayers helped me to finish this book.

To Father Ronald Lengwin and Father Angelus, I am so appreciative that they took the time out of their busy schedule to read a book by an author they did not know. I am inspired by their faith commitment, and grateful for their endorsements.

To Abby Barr who did the wonderful illustrations. I know the hand of God inspired her work.

To my niece, Lisa Marie Olshefski, who drew the gift boxes for the title page.

To my friend, John Bober who photographed the cover for me and taught me how to smile for the camera!

To the owner of Sincerely Yours, Inc. who allowed us to crawl inside his window space and capture a few of the many gift boxes that grace the front of his store in downtown Pittsburgh, PA. I pass his shop on the way to church in the morning and I love to gaze at all those beautifully wrapped gift boxes. After meeting the owner, I now know why. They were lovingly wrapped for God.

To all my friends, especially those at GNC (you know who you are), who put up with me every day, and to my family who have put up with me all of my life. I love you all.

Copyright Information:

Several years before the writing of this book, I awoke early one morning and was inspired to do a scripture study on prayer. I reached for my beloved Bible, a gift from a high school retreat. Using the doctrinal bible index in the back of my bible, I looked up each verse that was listed under the heading of "Prayer". After reviewing the scriptures and summarizing them, I wrote a short meditation on them. Little did I realize at the time, but that document was to become the foundation for this book.

You'll find the verses that are paraphrased in the first four chapters are from my original study and were summarized from:

> *St Joseph's Edition of the New American Bible,* translated from the Original Languages with Critical Use of All the Ancient Sources by Members of the Catholic Biblical Association of America, copyright © 1970, by Confraternity of Christian Doctrine, Washington, DC

> All scriptures quotations are taken from the HOLY BIBLE, NEW INTERNATIONAL VERSION®. Copyright © 1973, 1978, 1984 International Bible Society. All rights reserved.

Dedication

I would like to dedicate this book, first to my loving husband and soul mate George, who is an answer to an early childhood prayer. Also to all my friends, family and co-workers who are in my prayer box daily, and I thank those of you who have lovingly placed me in yours. And finally, to the Holy Spirit, who has inspired me to write this book. May God receive all the glory now and forever!

Preface

So what qualifies me to write a book on prayer? I have thought about that quite a bit lately since deciding to write this book and the primary reason I can think of is that *I pray*. I pray regularly. Likewise, I have studied what the Bible has to say about prayer. I have prayed from a very young age, and all of my prayers have been answered. I'm not trying to seem self-righteous when I say that all of my prayers have been answered, but they have. Sometimes God just says "No!" I do know God hears all of my prayers, perhaps, more precisely, all of *our* prayers. I have believed that without a doubt since I was a very young girl.

I don't know if that makes me qualified to write a book on prayer, but I have wanted to write it for a very long time. And so what follows is my book, a prayer box full of thoughts, prayers, poems, insights and inspirations. I hope it will inspire you to pray more. If you have never prayed, I hope it will encourage you to start praying, and will help you in your understanding of the gift of prayer, His gift to us, and our prayers, a gift to Him.

As we present our needs to God,

Let us wrap them in a gift box of praise and

Line it with tissue paper of thanksgiving and trust.

Enfold it with magnificent wrappings of adoration,

Lovingly tape it with confidence,

Unselfishly tie it with ribbons of hope,

Instantly cut the strands of doubt and anxiety, and

Adoringly offer our Gift lovingly and entirely to God.

Alleluia!

1

The Gift of Prayer

One morning as I was brushing my teeth, these words came to me. I ran to get a piece of paper and a pen to write them down. I pictured my prayers as a gift I wanted to present to God. This idea of putting our prayers in a box and giving them to God was the subject of a talk I heard at a conference of Christian working women.

The speaker talked about giving our prayer concerns completely to God and freeing ourselves from worry over those concerns. She said many of us do not let go of our troubles. Instead, we worry about the things we have placed in God's hands, not really letting go of them at all. We keep taking them back by worrying. She also suggested that we should place our loved ones in a box and give them completely to God, figuratively speaking, of course. That image has stuck with me.

At that same conference, I attended a session on prayer journalizing. I had started a prayer journal years before, but wasn't very consistent in writing my prayers. After this session, I decided to give it a try and began to write in a prayer journal on regular basis. I now have over ten journals filled with my prayers to God. Writing my prayers in a journal helps me to be more focused as I pray. It helps me to center on the Lord and let go of my concerns. Once I've written my conversation with God on the pages of my journal, I am able to visualize them in His almighty hands.

I am very open about my praying and as a result many people ask me to pray for them. I began drawing boxes, little gift boxes, in my journal. Inside these boxes, I write initials or names of those for whom I am praying. Many of my co-workers ask me to

place them in my prayer box regularly. When someone tells me that they have a problem or situation that they are concerned about, I tell them I will put them in my prayer box, and I do.

When I pray, I start by praising God; I ask him for forgiveness of my sins; I give thanks for all the blessings He has given me and then I present my needs to Him. Sometimes I list them in detail, and sometimes I just put initials in those little boxes all over the pages of my journal. I usually write one or two pages of praise and prayer in the morning before I start my day.

It is so important to consult with God on a regular basis throughout the day, but starting the morning in prayer is absolutely essential. It is like consulting with our heavenly CEO before delving into any major projects for that day. God gives us direction, inspiration, comfort, and love.

Have you ever considered what a gift God has given us, in the form of prayer? Prayer allows us to communicate with God, to confide in Him, and to enter into an intimate relationship with Him. Prayer fills us with perfect peace, security and hope. The results of prayer are limitless because God's powers know no bounds. He tells us to ask and we shall receive. Prayer truly is a gift from God.

Have you ever thought of your prayers as a gift to God? Scripture suggests that our prayers *"come like incense before*

God." (Psalm 141:2) How pleasing they must be to Him! We are also reminded in the first letter of John, chapter 3, verses 22-23:

We receive from God whatever we ask when we keep His commands and do what is pleasing to Him. So you see, it pleases God when we pray. God not only desires our prayers, He commands us to pray.

In Philippians 4:6, Paul reminds us not to be anxious about anything, but to pray about everything and be thankful for His provision.

Prayer is a powerful conversation with God. As you speak, He listens. When you are silent, He will speak to your heart, and you will know He has heard you. He may speak words of wisdom or you may just feel His loving, peaceful presence. His Spirit comes down upon us like a soft cloud with dew that caresses our cheeks and refreshes our soul with His love. Prayer is an unbroken circle of love between the Creator and His creation. As you offer your prayers to Him, He receives them as a gift and His blessings are given in return, and the gift of prayer continues.

Remember, as you present your needs to God, *wrap them in a gift box of praise lined with tissue paper of thanksgiving and trust. Enfold it with magnificent wrappings of adoration, tape it with confidence, and tie it with ribbons of hope as you cut the strands of doubt and anxiety, and offer it lovingly and entirely to God.* Don't forget to let go, and don't take your gift back by worrying. Let it rest in God's hands.

Into My Father's Arms

Mary Ann Haslett

When I was but a little girl
As bedtime would draw near,
My mother would call to me
to come and say my prayers.

When she called my siblings
They humbly would obey.
But I would grab my blanket,
And run the other way.

Into my father's lap I'd climb
And snuggle in his arms.
For there it was I felt secure,
safe from worldly harms.

Now many years have come and gone
Since my childhood days.
And as I have grown, I have changed
My simple, childish ways.

Through the years my faith has grown
As my parents taught me to believe
There is a God in whom we trust
His blessings daily we receive.

He is our heavenly Father,
Who sent his only Son
He died to save us from our sins
We are in Him made one.

From Calvary he rose triumphant,
and to the Father He returned.
But He left with us His Spirit.
And in the Trinity we are reborn.

So now when I seek comfort,
Peace, Joy, and a loving embrace,
Into my Father's arms I run,
And seek His Heavenly grace.

2

Childhood Prayers

When did I first learn to pray? As my poem illustrates, when I was very young, every evening, my mother would call us to pray. Now my dad would be in the living room in his favorite chair watching TV. I was about three or four years old at the time. My mother would gather us to go into the bedroom and kneel by the bed to pray. My older brother and sister were twins, born on her birthday. I don't know if it was because of this special bond they shared with Mom that they were so obedient or if it was because they were a little older than I was. I just know that I would rather be snuggling in my father's arms with my blanket.

I don't think it was because I didn't want to pray. It was probably because I might have been a bit too young to understand what prayer was. Also at that age, I found my dad's lap to be more comfortable than kneeling on the hard, cold floor. But I do remember how we used to pray. It went something like this:

"God bless Grandma and Grandpa, Mommy and Daddy, Carol, Eddie and Mary Ann ..." and so we continued naming all of our uncles and aunts, and every other living relative we could remember. Once we finished the litany of names, we would pray the traditional prayers "Our Father," "Hail Mary" and the "Glory Be" that Mom had also taught us as soon as we could talk.

I grew up in the late '50s and early '60s in a traditional Catholic family. We went to mass every Sunday and Holy Day, we all went to Catholic School for our elementary education, we didn't eat meat on Fridays during Lent, and we went to confession frequently. So not only did my mom teach us to pray, we were taught about our faith each and every school day from those loving women in black habits affectionately known as "Nuns."

I loved Catholic school. I loved going to Mass every day and I knew faith was important from an early age. I remember one of my childhood prayers I prayed "Don't let me become a nun." I don't know why I didn't want to become a nun. Maybe it was those black habits that covered all but the hands and the face. I was such a tomboy and thought that those habits would be way to confining when I traipse through the woods and up and down hills and climb trees. Knowing me as He does, God agreed with that prayer.

My parents were older when they got married and it was the first marriage for both of them. They were dealing with the pressure of raising three small children. My father had a temper, and when my mom and dad would fight, I would run to my room and kneel down by my bed and cover my ears and pray that they would stop fighting. I also remember praying that God would bless me with a good man to love and who would love me in return. I know it seems like a peculiar thing for a child to pray, but honestly, I did. At the age of 26, I can undoubtedly say the Lord answered that prayer perfectly. I love to pleasantly remind my husband that he was the answer to the first prayer I ever remember praying.

Now there were two other events that happened when I was a child. I truly believe that these were amazing answers to prayer.

My mother's parents were immigrants from Poland, and Grandma spoke only Polish, and Grandpa spoke Polish, some broken English and a bit of German. They lived in a big old house that wasn't too far from our house. In their later years, they were still able to live by themselves with the help of my mom and her brothers. When I was in third grade, Grandpa contracted pneumonia, ended up in the hospital, and shortly thereafter, on a cold March day, died at the age of 87.

Now I remember my mom worrying about what was to become of Grandma. She was 90 years old, and it would be difficult for her to stay alone in her own home. I am sure when Mom knelt down the night her father died, as she always did to pray, she asked God for His help. I remember lying in bed concerned about it too since I knew Mom was worried over the care of her mother. I don't remember if I actually asked God for His help that night, but I am positive I had a conversation with God about it. God knew what was on our hearts, and on the day of Grandpap's funeral, Grandma also died of pneumonia. I do remember thinking that God certainly knew what He was doing. More recently, I've perceived that my grandparents' timely deaths were an answer to our unspoken prayers.

The very next year, right before Christmas, a very young cousin of mine died in an extremely sad mishap. I remember being quite afraid of dying and as I lay awake in bed one night I talked to God about my fears. I told Him I was afraid to die, and asked Him to comfort me. I fell into a deep sleep and I had an extraordinary dream of a splendid place. I remember rolling green hills of grass and gardens of flowers that were so lovely I wanted to remain in that dream forever. It was so real, I knew when I woke up God had answered my simple prayer. I have always felt it was a glimpse of heaven because I have never been afraid to die since. Now when I read in scripture the description of our heavenly Home I know that He has prepared a place for us more magnificent than we could ever ask or imagine.

In the book of Revelation, Chapter 21 describes the heavenly city of Jerusalem. In verses 10 and 11, John was taken in spirit to a great high mountain and shown "the holy city Jerusalem coming down out of heaven from God. It gleamed with the splendor of God. The city had the radiance of a precious jewel that sparkled like a diamond."

In verses 18 through 21, the city was described as having walls decorated with a rainbow of colorful precious stones including jasper, sapphire, emerald, topaz, and amethyst. The twelve gates were made of pearls and the streets of the city were of pure gold, transparent as glass.

I can't wait to see the splendor of heaven and all those precious stones with all their brilliant color, the shiny gold streets and pearly white gates.

I am confident that my loved ones, who have already died, believing that Jesus died for their sins, have found their rest in His heavenly home.

"In the same way, the Spirit helps us in our weakness. We do not know what we ought to pray for, but the Spirit himself intercedes for us with groans that words cannot express. And he who searches our hearts knows the mind of the Spirit, because the Spirit intercedes for the saints in accordance with God's will.

And we know that in all things God works for the good of those who love him, who have been called according to his purpose."

Romans 8:26–28

3

God's Word on Prayer

Seeking God for His direction in our prayers is essential. After all, we are entering into communion with Him as we converse with our Lord. Therefore, it is important that we consult His Word to learn from Him how we should pray.

So what does scripture say about prayer? First, it teaches us that *we don't even know how to pray,* so we must seek the Holy Spirit for His intercession. I read from Romans 8 when I was a senior in high school and it really spoke to my heart. It reminded me that I don't need to know how to pray correctly, I just need to talk to God and the Holy Spirit will help me, even if I don't know the right words to say.

Therefore if the Spirit prays for us with inexpressible groans, we shouldn't be too concerned about using eloquent words or perfect speeches, God knows our heart. Even if we forget to pray about something, He doesn't. He knows what is on our mind. Therefore, we can't pray incorrectly, as long as we are sincere, and believe in Him who hears us pray. This is fundamental: We must trust when we pray that he hears, and He does, because He says He does.

Scripture also teaches us the fundamentals of prayer. Jesus himself taught us to pray with confidence in Matthew 6:8–15, in the words of the "Our Father." What can we learn about prayer in the words of Jesus?

"Our Father, who art in heaven, hallowed be thy name . . ."

He taught us to call God "Our Father" and to praise His name. Think about the intimacy of being a child of God! Since He instructs us to call Him our Father, we are His children, and He must want what is best for us. Don't our parents want us to be happy, and give us good things? So much more so our heavenly Father wants us to enjoy the gifts He so lovingly bestows on us. Just like any parents He also lovingly disciplines us so to help us become better children.

"Thy kingdom come, thy will be done, on earth as it is in heaven . . ."

We implore God's will to be done in our lives. We look forward to the coming of His Heavenly Kingdom, our eternal home.

"Give us this day our daily bread . . ."

We ask for God's providential care to supply all of our needs.

"Forgive us our trespasses as we forgive those who trespass against us . . ."

We ask for forgiveness of our sins, and are taught to forgive others too.

"Lead us not into temptation, but deliver us from evil . . ."

We ask God to help us with the battle of sin and temptation.

Jesus again showed us an important element of prayer

when He raised Lazarus from the dead. He called upon His Father in this way:

> *"Father, I thank you that you have heard me. I knew that you always hear me, but I said this for the benefit of the people standing here, that they may believe that you sent me."*
>
> John 11:41b–42

He thanked the Father for having heard Him, this implies two things about prayer: First, Jesus acknowledged that God had heard Him and this suggests God hears us when we pray, thus giving us confidence when we pray, believing God hears us. In other words, Jesus is teaching us to have faith in God because He does hear our prayers.

And second, it also teaches us to give God thanks for hearing us, and to thank Him for answering our prayers.

Scripture also reminds us to pray often, teaching us when, where and how to pray. In these verses we are reminded the true power and importance of prayer. In Matthew we read:

> *"Ask and it will be given to you; seek and you will find; knock and the door will be opened to you. For everyone who asks receives; he who seeks finds; and to him who knocks, the door will be opened.*
> *. . . how much more will your Father in heaven give good gifts to those who ask him! ."*
>
> Matthew 7:7–8, 11b

Again in Matthew, we are encouraged to have faith, truly believing that God can do all things:

> *" . . . I tell you the truth, if you have faith as small as a mustard seed, you can say to this moun-*

tain, 'Move from here to there' and it will move.
Nothing will be impossible for you."

Matthew 17:20

Jesus instructs us to come together in prayer. How often we come together to meet, to talk, to gossip, or to complain about our circumstances. If only we would spend more time in prayer together. Jesus tells us He will be with us:

"Again, I tell you that if two of you on earth agree
about anything you ask for, it will be done for
you by my Father in heaven. For where two or
three come together in my name, there am I with
them."

Matthew 18:19–20

In the Gospel of Luke 18:1, we are instructed to pray always and not lose hope. This verse declares that prayer should be an integral part of our day. I talk to God anywhere. When I see a beautiful sunset, or a bright red cardinal sitting on a carpet of fresh white snow in my backyard, or two graceful fawns grazing in a field, or the majestic view from high atop a mountain, I praise Him and thank Him for His marvelous creation. When I have a problem or need insight into a situation, I call upon Him wherever I am, at my desk at work, on the bus or in a grocery line. It doesn't matter where I am, I know He hears me. Because I feel His comfort and presence, and many times His answers come in the wink of an eye. The phone will ring or someone will pass by with just the information I am looking for. And I know He heard and He answered. Why? Because I asked in His name as He commanded, and He answered as He said He would. In John 14:14, Jesus tells us to ask anything in His name and He will do it.

It sounds so simple, but that is what childlike faith is all about, trusting God, as you did when you were a child. Why is it when we become adults we have a tendency to lose that childlike faith? I guess it is because God gave us the gift of free will, and when we are old enough to make decisions for ourselves, we begin to make them all by ourselves, and forget that God is always there to help. Just like when a child is learning how to do something for the first time. Once they have learned it, they don't want their parents helping them anymore. So too it is with us, we can do it without any help. But I have found, God knows best and He who created all wants us to call upon Him for His help.

He also teaches us to abide in him and follow his word, and when we abide in Him we can be assured that what we ask will be done for us. (John 15:7)

Another scripture assures us that God hears us:

> *"This is the confidence we have in approaching God: that if we ask anything according to his will, he hears us."*
>
> 1 John 5:14

In Ephesians 6:18 we are instructed:

> *"And pray in the Spirit on all occasions with all kinds of prayers and requests. With this in mind, be alert and always keep on praying for all the saints. "*

The first letter of Timothy urges us about whom we should pray for:

> *"I urge, then, first of all, that requests, prayers, intercession and thanksgiving be made for everyone— for kings and all those in authority,*

that we may live peaceful and quiet lives in all godliness and holiness. This is good, and pleases God our Savior, who wants all men to be saved and to come to a knowledge of the truth. For there is one God and one mediator between God and men, the man Christ Jesus, who gave himself as a ransom for all men—the testimony given in its proper time."

1 Timothy 2:1–6

This message is especially important for all of us, because it is God's will that all men should be saved. Also we are reminded to pray for those in authority, especially during these troubled times. There is a wonderful Web site that has been created and it encourages us to pray for our government leaders. It is *www.presidentialprayerteam.org* and it is a great way to help us to remember to follow Paul's advice to Timothy to pray for those in authority.

We are shown many examples of answer to prayers in Scripture as in James 5:16–18:

> *"Therefore confess your sins to each other and pray for each other so that you may be healed. The prayer of a righteous man is powerful and effective.*
>
> *Elijah was a man just like us. He prayed earnestly that it would not rain, and it did not rain on the land for three and a half years. Again he prayed, and the heavens gave rain, and the earth produced its crops."*

Following the example of Elijah, whenever we are going on a trip or planning an outdoor event, I always consult with God on the weather, for He is in control. We are most frequently blessed with the appropriate weather for the occasion. The Bible was written for us, as an example to us. It is an instruction book on life, and each verse that was written is intended for our benefit.

There are also many references to prayer in the Old Testament. These examples are beautiful reminders to us: In Sirach 7:10, we are reminded not to be impatient in prayers.

Again in Sirach 35:16-18 we learn that the one who serves God willing will be heard. His prayers will pierce the clouds and be heard by our heavenly Father. He will judge fairly and respond accordingly to the righteous.

So then, what can we conclude about prayer? Jesus teaches us to pray by praising God, asking Him for forgiveness, presenting our needs before Him, and finally, thanking Him for His goodness. I once read that complete prayer should include these same four ingredients, using the acronym *"PART"* to define them:

P: Praise God: Give Him all the Glory and Honor and Praise!

A: Admission of sins: Confess our faults and weaknesses.

R: Requests: Present our needs and requests to Him.

T: Thanks: Give Him thanks for hearing and answering us!

Let's do our *"PART"* and pray the way God has lovingly taught us.

There is another similar acronym, *"ACTS"*:

A: Adoration: Worship Him with love, exalt His Holy Name!

C: Confession: Admit your sins and offenses

T: Thanksgiving: Thank Him for His abundant blessings

S: Supplication: Humbly ask Him for His generous provisions.

In summary then, what has God taught us about prayer?

- ❖ To pray always.
- ❖ To ask in His name.
- ❖ To believe that He has heard us when we ask.
- ❖ We don't even know how to pray, but the Holy Spirit will intercede for us.
- ❖ To pray for each other and those in authority.
- ❖ And as the "Our Father" teaches:
  - · Praise Him.
  - · His will be done.
  - · Ask for His provision.
  - · Ask forgiveness and forgive others.
  - · Ask Him to keep us from Evil.

"*I urge, then, first of all, that requests, prayers, intercession and thanksgiving be made for everyone— for kings and all those in authority, that we may live peaceful and quiet lives in all godliness and holiness. This is good, and pleases God our Savior, who wants all men to be saved and to come to a knowledge of the truth. For there is one God and one mediator between God and men, the man Christ Jesus, who gave Himself as a ransom for all men—the testimony given in its proper time.*"

1 Timothy 2:1–6

4

Intercessory Prayer

Intercessory prayer can be defined as the act of prayer, petition or entreaty in favor of another, in other words, praying for each other. As we again read in Paul's letter to Timothy, we see that our prayers offered for others can result in "tranquil" lives, and that these kinds of prayers are pleasing to God.

I remember when I was in Catholic school, for Mother's Day or Father's Day or other special occasions, we would make "Spiritual Bouquets." These creations were usually colorful construction paper cards with paper lace doilies in which we would inscribe words or poetry of love that included a list of prayers that we had offered for our loved ones. Not knowing it at the time, I was partaking in intercessory prayer. We were actually presenting our prayers as a gift to our parents and family. Just as prayer is a gift to God, and a gift from God, our prayer is certainly a gift to those for whom we pray.

We previously read in Ephesians 6:18, that we should pray for others every chance we get.

A good friend of mine was going through a terrible illness, she told me she was so sick she was unable to pray. At the time, I found that hard to believe. This is a lady that loves the Lord and prays all the time. She and her husband belong to a community of believers and even host an evening Bible study for couples. How could she not be able to pray? I just couldn't imagine that. But I didn't doubt it and we all prayed for her. I remember her telling us how much our prayers helped and she recovered completely from her illness.

Her illness helped me to see the importance of intercessory prayer. But I really learned it firsthand this past year as I was awaiting spinal surgery. Since I love to pray, and I pray for others, as well as myself, I wasn't in the habit of asking for prayer too often. I figured if I prayed for myself, there was no need to have others pray for the same things I was asking. I didn't understand the importance of others praying for me until I felt the effects of it.

Let me explain how that happened. I found out I was to have surgery in August, and by the time I had gone through all the tests, and doctor visits it wasn't until December that I finally had the surgery. With four months of waiting, I found myself having anxieties about the surgery, even though I knew that God has said not to be anxious about anything. I kept confessing my doubts, and even though I was praying, I was still having them. So I began to ask some friends and family to pray for me. Before I knew it, I was feeling that peace that surpasses all understanding, just as Paul describes in Philippians 4:6–7:

> *"Do not be anxious about anything, but in everything, by prayer and petition, with thanksgiving, present your requests to God. And the peace of God, which transcends all understanding, will guard your heart and your minds in Christ Jesus."*

It is really hard to describe just what that peace that surpasses all understanding feels like. If I were to try to describe it, it would be the feeling you get Christmas Eve on a clear, star-filled night with a gentle white snow falling covering the earth, surrounded by family, the fire glowing brightly in the fireplace. The chestnuts roasting on the open fire are optional. When I think of those old familiar Christmas carols and the feeling of peace they instill in our hearts, I guess the best way I can summarize it: a gentle calm, a blessed assurance, a peaceful night's sleep, the feeling that all is well.

I think when we pray for others, we build walls of protection around each other, keeping us safe from the snares of the evil one.

I remember after graduating from college I went through a desert time in my life. It is during those desert times that we really need intercessory prayer—when we can't pray for ourselves or are so thick in the middle of our problems that we can't see ourselves clear to get out.

After graduation, I felt that God had abandoned me, and I was alone in a desert. I had just finished the four most exhilarating years of my life, only to discover I had no clue what I wanted to do with the rest of my life. I had pursued a degree in education, but I really didn't feel qualified to teach.

There I was, back in my parents' home, under their watchful eye, after enjoying four years of independence. I was feeling dejected, uncertain about the future and mad at God. Why did He allow this to happen to me? Of course I blamed it on Him, not realizing that it was my own fault for not knowing that if I wanted to maintain my independence upon graduation, it was up to me to figure out what I really wanted to do with my life after having finished college. Unfortunately, for several months, I told God I was not going to talk to Him, I was mad at Him for letting this happen to me.

I didn't stop believing in Him, I just stopped talking to Him for a while. Thankfully, I was blessed with a praying family. I know of at least two cousins that told me they were praying for me and I am sure my mother was on her knees praying for me morning and night. Though at the time I didn't understand the power of intercessory prayer, I am sure it was their prayers that accompanied me through that desert time.

During that time, my brother was a lector at our church, meaning he read the readings for mass and lead the prayers of the faithful. Since it was the year of the family in our church, he invited me to attend a mass at his house for all the lectors. They were all married couples but they thought it would be nice if we would lector together as brother and sister. I had enjoyed being a lector in college at the mass for the students, so I looked forward to doing it again. Little did I realize that even though I had turned my back on God, He had not abandoned me. It is a privilege to proclaim the Word of God, and when you do it, you can't help but receive His blessings from reading it.

Even though I had stopped praying for a while, others were praying for me and God was working in my life. Through the grace of God, I ended up working for a local company as a cashier. Not long after, I landed a job in their computer department, where I met my husband. Through the encouragement of a dynamic boss and mentor I found a new career in programming that I would have never dreamed possible. God works in our lives when we ask Him, and our prayers impact the lives of those for whom we pray.

Two days before I was to have my second spinal surgery in ten years, I was at work, trying not to dwell on my impending ordeal. I had just gotten back from a meeting when a neighboring coworker asked me to pray for our secretary. She had just received word that her daughter was the victim of a gas explosion in her own home. She had two small children and they too were in the home when it exploded. I didn't know all of the details, but I immediately began to lift her up in prayer. I prayed that the Lord would protect her family and provide the care they needed. I prayed that our secretary would feel God's presence and strength as she drove to the hospital that he would give comfort to her and keep her calm. The next morning she confided that she had felt the effects of our prayers. She knew we were praying for her and her family. Her daughter had sustained third-degree burns to her hands, but her prognosis was good, her grandchildren were fine, and she felt the Lord's presence and His calming peace that surpasses all understanding as she raced to the hospital. Not surprisingly, I felt it too.

Finally, and probably the most difficult, we are instructed to intercede for our enemies as well, and for those who have offended us. Jesus tells us in Matthew 5:44–45 to " . . . *Love your enemies and pray for those who persecute you, that you may be sons of your Father in heaven. He causes his sun to rise on the evil and the good, and sends rain on the righteous and the unrighteous.*"

When we pray for them we should ask God to show us how to love them, and see them how He sees them, so that we might love and forgive them in the same way He does. In praying this way, we will be able to put an end to gossip and speaking unkindly of others, because He will show us the way to love and fill us with His love for them.

After all, we too have sinned and offended others. As we realize this, shouldn't we all need and want to be intercessors for each other?

Family Prayer

By Casey Alexa Peel

Every night I say a prayer
With my parents and my brothers,
We pray for the poor
And we pray for others.

God, please help the poor
And people in need
Listen to the family prayer
And feed the starved indeed.

God, please make us friends
And help us be kind to every boy and girl.
Teach us to help one another
And make a peaceful world.

God, please heal the injured
And cure the ill.
We should all be thankful
For the sharing of God's will.

Thank you, God for watching us
And for loving us too
Even when we don't obey
And act as you would do.

Amen!

*Author's Note: Casey, a budding young poet, is the daughter of my
dear friend. We are permanent residents in each other's prayer boxes.*

5

Family Prayer

I am sure you have heard of the old adage, "The family that prays together, stays together." I can attest to the fact that it does. My father's temper created a very stressful home environment, but my mother prayed continually for our family and even though I didn't understand it at the time, her prayers were the threads that bond our family together. My parents remained together throughout the years, when I know it would have been easier for my mother to walk out on the marriage. I will be forever grateful for my mother's faith and prayers. In the beginning she taught us to pray, and in the end, at my father's funeral, she taught me true love and forgiveness. When I commented that she wouldn't have to put up with his yelling anymore, she told me she only wanted to remember the good things about him.

I had always wanted to marry a man that would share my faith. When I first met my husband, he had never been baptized. He didn't even go to church. But there was something about him so loving and kind that I was instantly attracted to him and I knew we were meant to be together. He lived his life the way Jesus taught us to live. I, on the other hand, had a strong faith, but I struggled with some less-than-Christian personality flaws. He loved me anyway, and he was a great influence on my personality. I never tried to force my faith on him, but I did pray for him, and I always asked him if he wanted to go to church with me, and frequently he did. One day, six years after we were married, he told me he wanted to be baptized and join the church. I was so delighted when he made this decision. I know it was God's answer to my prayers.

Since that time, we have also joined a prayer group called "Couples for Christ." We meet on a weekly basis with other couples and we sing praises to God. We pray for each other, we study scripture, and we share how God is working in our lives. When we come together to worship in His name, He is in our midst. We experience His love and presence very deeply during these sessions. As we gather together I am reminded of what Jesus professed:

> *"Again, I tell you that if two of you on earth agree about anything you ask for, it will be done for you by my Father in heaven. For where two or three come together in my name, there am I with them."*
>
> Matthew 18:19–20

So it pleases God when we seek Him together. He protects and guides and blesses us. In 1 Peter 3:12, we are reminded:

> *"For the eyes of the Lord are on the righteous and his ears are attentive to their prayer, but the face of the Lord is against those who do evil."*

Also we should continually forgive each other for our failings and pray for each other as we are instructed in James 5:16:

> *"Therefore confess your sins to each other and pray for each other so that you may be healed.*

The prayer of a righteous man is powerful and effective."

If our prayers are powerful and effective, shouldn't we try to pray more together as a family?

"He has showed you, O man, what is good. And what does the LORD require of you? To act justly and to love mercy and to walk humbly with your God."

Micah 6:8

6

Walking with God in Prayer

How can we walk humbly with our God? In college, not long after I first read Romans chapter eight and discovered a personal relationship with the Lord, I would walk to class and privately converse with Him as I went. Sometimes I would ask Him for help on a test, or thank Him for the beauty of the morning, or just glorify Him for His goodness. I shared with Him my deepest thoughts, and at that age we have so many deep thoughts! College was a whole new adventure for me. I loved it, and I was involved in so many activities and the college campus where I went was very spread out. So I did a lot of walking and thus I had a lot of alone time to spend with God in prayer as I walked to class or to my early morning job at the library. Whether I was walking to a sporting event, or going to class, or going to church or the cafeteria, if someone wasn't walking with me, I was walking with God including Him on my every thought and asking His direction for my every action.

Proverbs 3:5–6 tells us to:

> *"Trust in the LORD with all your heart and lean not on your own understanding; in all your ways acknowledge him, and he will make your paths straight."*

I don't remember the first time I heard this scripture,

but I think it was the very first verse I memorized. It is one of my very favorite scriptures. I quote it frequently, as a reminder that we are to acknowledge God in ALL ways. He cares about every thing that happens to us, even the little stuff. Sometimes I think, especially the little stuff, because when we confide in Him about everything it indicates that we have established a deep, loving relationship with Him, the kind that is reserved for best friends. I believe that it delights God when we look to Him as a loving friend in whom we want to share all our joys, all our sorrows, all our hopes and fears. After all, He created us. He loves us and numbers every hair on our head. Everything that happens to us is important to Him.

Having a relationship with the Lord that encompasses every aspect of my life gives me great joy and an abundance of blessings. I am so grateful to God for all the blessings in my life.

One of my greatest joys is receiving the Lord in communion. On the night before Jesus died for us, He instituted the rite of Holy Communion. In the first letter of Paul to the Corinthians, chapter 11 and verses 23 through 26,

> *"The Lord Jesus, on the night he was betrayed, took bread, and when he had given thanks, he broke it and said, 'This is my body, which is for you; do this in remembrance of me.' In the same way, after supper he took the cup, saying, 'This cup is the new covenant in my blood; do this, whenever you drink it, in remembrance of me.' For whenever you eat this bread and drink this cup, you proclaim the Lord's death until he comes."*

I personally believe Jesus chose bread and wine to become His body and blood because of how it makes us feel. Bread is a comfort food that we enjoy eating. It is satisfying and filling to eat. Wine gives a warm and joyful feeling as we sip it. I think that is how Jesus wanted us to experience His presence with us—in a warm, comforting and joyful way.

"*Very early in the morning, while it was still dark, Jesus got up, left the house and went off to a solitary place, where he prayed.*"

Mark 1:35

7

My Prayer Chair

Just as Jesus sought a solitary place to pray, I have a prayer chair that I go to very early in the morning. It is a chaise lounge, part of a sectional living room set. When I am awakened early in the morning, I'll go there to pray. Sometimes it is as early as 3:30 A.M. Usually, I'll stretch out, and begin to pray. Many times I fall asleep, but it is always a very restful sleep. I feel like I am resting in God's arms. I'm always at peace in my prayer chair. I feel His presence so strongly there. Sometimes, I'll read a scripture that speaks to my heart and inspires me. It is my alone place with God.

Perhaps we can hear God better in the silence of the early morning, or perhaps He prefers to speak to us in the quiet hours of the day. Sometimes He calls out in the middle of the night, as in 1 Samuel 3:3-4, the Lord called to Samuel. *'The lamp of God had not yet gone out,' and Samuel was lying down in the temple of the LORD , where the ark of God was. Then the LORD called Samuel. Samuel answered, 'Here I am.'"*

In 1 King 19:11-13 the Lord appeared to Elijah: *"'Go out and stand on the mountain in the presence of the LORD, for the LORD is about to pass by.'*

Then a great and powerful wind tore the mountains apart and shattered the rocks before the LORD , but the LORD was not in the wind. Af-

ter the wind there was an earthquake, but the LORD was not in the earthquake. After the earthquake came a fire, but the LORD was not in the fire. And after the fire came a gentle whisper. When Elijah heard it, he pulled his cloak over his face and went out and stood at the mouth of the cave."

The Lord didn't reveal himself in the earthquake or the fire but in a gentle whisper. We need the quiet hours to spend time with Him so we can hear His gentle whisper and respond, "Here I am, Lord." When the Lord calls us in the wee small hours of the day, we should respond to His call, just as Samuel did. Perhaps He just wants to spend quiet time with us to refresh and bless us. It is not easy to get out of bed to respond to His call, but when I do, I am always blessed and frequently enlightened with His wisdom. He hears us in the silence of the morning, without ever having to speak a word, He reads those words engraved on our hearts and responds with His loving and peaceful embrace.

Treasured pictures that reveal insights into the beauty, peace and love of God surround my prayer chair.

Across from my chair is a black-and-white picture of Jesus. An artist wrote the gospel of John in such a way that it forms Jesus' face with the words written in different intensities of black and gray. What a work of art it is! I love to look upon His face as I pray.

I also have three Thomas Kincade pictures that are on the wall beside my chair. One is called *The Bridge of Faith*, with one of the most comforting scriptures John 14:1–4,6.

"'Do not let your hearts be troubled. Trust in God; trust also in me. In my Father's house are many rooms; if it were not so, I would have told you. I

am going there to prepare a place for you. And if I go and prepare a place for you, I will come back and take you to be with me that you also may be where I am. You know the way to the place where I am going.'

Jesus answered, 'I am the way and the truth and the life. No one comes to the Father except through me.'"

The other is a *Garden of Prayer*, a beautiful gazebo in a lovely garden of brightly colored flowers and foliage.

And the third is a small fishing cottage with a small pier next to a small stream. It contains the verse:

"'Come, follow me,' Jesus said, 'and I will make you fishers of men.'"

Matthew 4:19

I also have a sweet picture of a kitten lying on a Bible soundly sleeping beside a gold fish in a small round fishbowl watching intently. The words "He comforts us with his love" appear at the bottom of the picture. That is how I feel when I am curled up in His arms in my prayer chair. I love to bask in the warmth of His love.

I am sure others have sensed His peaceful presence there too. My dear uncle has fallen so soundly asleep in my prayer chair, I can't help but think he has experienced that perfect peace resting in God's arms. My sister-in-law seeks out my chair to find some peaceful rest after a busy holiday. And when I make my morning visit to my chair to pray, I have a cat that immediately comes to rest upon my lap. As my cat curls up and settles in, I find a connection and comfort in her peaceful and trusting existence. Just as she rests in my lap, I imagine myself resting in His arms.

Psalm 91

He who dwells in the shelter of the Most High
will rest in the shadow of the Almighty.
I will say of the LORD , "He is my refuge and my fortress,
my God, in whom I trust."

Surely he will save you from the fowler's snare
and from the deadly pestilence.
He will cover you with his feathers,
and under his wings you will find refuge;
his faithfulness will be your shield and rampart.
You will not fear the terror of night,
nor the arrow that flies by day,
nor the pestilence that stalks in the darkness,
nor the plague that destroys at midday . . .

If you make the Most High your dwelling-
even the LORD, who is my refuge-
then no harm will befall you,
no disaster will come near your tent.
For he will command his angels concerning you
to guard you in all your ways;
they will lift you up in their hands,
so that you will not strike your foot against a stone.
You will tread upon the lion and the cobra;
you will trample the great lion and the serpent.

"Because he loves me," says the LORD , "I will rescue him;
I will protect him, for he acknowledges my name.
He will call upon me, and I will answer him;
I will be with him in trouble,
I will deliver him and honor him.
With long life will I satisfy him
and show him my salvation."

8

Answered Prayers and Blessings from God

Over the years, God has blessed me so abundantly that it is hard to enumerate all of them, but there have been several birthday gifts I have received at the hands of God and they are always so special.

In 1992 I had my first spinal surgery. I was diagnosed with tethered cord, a congenital malformation of the spinal cord. My spinal cord was longer than normal, and it was tethered by fibrous tumors that had to be detached with a laser knife. That first surgery was unexpected, but it was to be a significant faith building experience. The whole time I was in the hospital I felt that God covered me with His healing blanket of love. I felt His presence so closely as I went through a total recovery.

While I was in the hospital, a minister of the Eucharist brought me Holy Communion. I was so overwhelmed by the Lord's presence, and I so appreciated someone coming each day that I was in the hospital to bring me communion, that I asked God if it be His will, that I could share in this ministry.

Less than two years later, on my birthday, I became a lay minister at our local hospital. It was such a wonderful birthday gift. It brings me great joy and many blessings as I continue my ministry of distributing communion to the sick.

One year on my birthday, my husband and I went to a bed and breakfast that had the theme of "Gone with the Wind." It was such a lovely birthday weekend, and on the morning of my birthday, I awoke very early to pray. I went to the library that faced the east, and during my prayer time I experienced the most beautiful sunrise, the sky was shades of purple and pink so lovely that I am sure God painted them that morning just for my birthday.

Last year for my birthday, I took a "ladies only" trip with my sister and two cousins. We went to the Bahamas the week of my birthday. The whole trip we had the most beautiful weather imaginable. Everything from the flight down to the resort, to our rooms, to our meals, to our activities was absolutely perfect. I know that God had truly blessed each moment of that birthday trip.

My faith has grown over the years because of some of the ways God has answered prayers. I try not to put God in "the prayer box" when I pray. Let me illustrate what I mean by that. Once I had a large amount of photocopying that needed done for a class I was teaching the next day at work. The photocopier in our department was not working and so I called the corporate copy department, but they were so backlogged they would be unable to do my job in time for the class. So I began to pray. I asked God to free up some time for my job at the corporate copy center. I went into elaborate detail about how He should bless them so they could get their work down so they could do my copying. The afternoon passed, the next morning came and I still did not have my copies made. I kept telling God I trusted Him advising Him how He could help me. Then at the zero hour, the department secretary came over to me and said that the copy repairman had come to fix our copier, and he needed something to copy to make sure it was working correctly. I gave her my materials to be copied, and the repairman made all the copies I needed in time for the class! I learned a valuable lesson that day. I didn't need to tell God how to answer my prayer, I simply needed to tell Him what I needed and He supplied it in His most perfect way. His will for our lives is so much more perfect than we could ever ask or imagine, as we are told in Ephesians 3:20–21:

> *"Now to him who is able to do immeasurably more than all we ask or imagine, according to his power that is at work within us, to him be glory in the church and in Christ Jesus through-out all generations, for ever and ever! Amen."*

Since Paul reminds us in his letter to the Philippians not to be anxious about anything, but in all things pray, I have always tried not to be anxious about anything. The second time I found out I had to have spinal surgery to de-tether my spinal cord, it took four months for the surgery to be scheduled, I had a lot of time to contemplate it.

One of the thoughts that plagued me was "I don't even know this surgeon" and "I've never been in this hospital." I wondered if the surgery would be as success-ful as it had been the first time with a different surgeon in a different hospital.

The Sunday before my surgery was scheduled, I took communion to our local hospital, and the first room I went into was a young woman. I asked her how she was feeling, and she replied that she was hoping to go home that day. I said, "I'll be in your shoes next Sunday won-dering the same thing. I'm having surgery Friday." She inquired where the surgery was to take place and who the surgeon was. When I told her, she stated **that he had been her surgeon** and she had surgery just one year ago in that same hospital. The operation had been a success and she had had a pleasant experience with the hospi-tal. Isn't God wonderful? He sent me an angel to squelch that anxious thought. I truly rested in that peace that transcends all understanding.

My first appointment to meet with the surgeon was in late September. I was told that he planned on using a new laser pen that he had heard about at a conference only the week before. This was God's timing, no doubt. This pen was to prevent adhesions, and my spinal cord had been stuck in the adhesions from the last surgery. So I knew God's hand had been in the timing of my appointment and the conference.

In the months prior to surgery, I had plenty of time to wonder if the surgeon had gotten the laser pen, and if he had read the manual on it, and most importantly if he had practiced using it on anyone else. I kept confessing my anxiety, but those questions kept coming to my mind. Finally the day came. God put my mind at ease. Shortly before my operation, my doctor entered pre-op and introduced me to another surgeon from Johns Hopkins University, an expert in the use of that laser pen would be assisting with my surgery!

My surgery was to begin at 2:30 PM. I had told my husband that he and my siblings should go to get something to eat around 4 PM because that would be about half way through the four hour operation. I wanted to make sure they would find time to get some rest and nourishment during those hours of waiting. As I lay on the gurney in the pre-op, I watched the hands of the clock move slowly past the hour of three and then four. "Oh God" I prayed, "please let them know that my surgery hasn't begun yet. I don't want them to be worrying as they must wait for two additional hours". My heart was heavy for them, because of the stress of prolonged waiting they would endure. My part was easy, they'd put me to sleep and I'd wake up in the recovery room to their anxious eyes. When I awoke, it was 8:30, my husband related to me that my surgery took two hours less than was planned. Before I told him I had been praying that they would know my surgery was delayed, I asked if they had eaten. He told to me that they had, and that when they got on one of the many elevators in this very large university hospital, who got on the elevator right after they did but my surgeon. When George introduced himself and asked him wasn't he supposed to be operating on me, my doctor told him my surgery was delayed and remarked it was a good time for them to get something to eat! What an awesome answer to my prayer! The surgery was a success and I thank God for His loving and healing hand upon me.

Sometimes the blessings God provides are in His word that speaks to us and gives us His peace. Prior to my first surgery I was confessing anxious thoughts and prayed for his blessed assurance that all would be well. I remember turning to Psalm 139. It has become one of my favorites, and I know it was God speaking directly to me of my concerns:

O LORD , you have searched me and you know me.
You know when I sit and when I rise;
you perceive my thoughts from afar.
You discern my going out and my lying down;
you are familiar with all my ways.
Before a word is on my tongue
you know it completely, O LORD .

You hem me in-behind and before;
you have laid your hand upon me.
Such knowledge is too wonderful for me,
too lofty for me to attain.
Where can I go from your Spirit?
Where can I flee from your presence?
If I go up to the heavens, you are there;
if I make my bed in the depths, you are there.

If I rise on the wings of the dawn,
if I settle on the far side of the sea,
even there your hand will guide me,
your right hand will hold me fast.

If I say, "Surely the darkness will hide me
and the light become night around me,"
even the darkness will not be dark to you;
the night will shine like the day,
for darkness is as light to you.

For you created my inmost being;
you knit me together in my mother's womb.
I praise you because I am fearfully and wonderfully
made;
your works are wonderful,
I know that full well.
My frame was not hidden from you
when I was made in the secret place.
When I was woven together in the depths of the earth,
your eyes saw my unformed body.
All the days ordained for me
were written in your book
before one of them came to be.

How precious to me are your thoughts, O God!
How vast is the sum of them!
Were I to count them,
they would outnumber the grains of sand.
When I awake,
I am still with you....

Search me, O God, and know my heart;
test me and know my anxious thoughts.
See if there is any offensive way in me,
and lead me in the way everlasting.

I was having nasal surgery recently and was calmly reading a devotional booklet as I awaited the surgery, and what scripture should be included in that booklet as a loving reminder again? Not surprisingly, Psalm 139! I smiled and knew He was with me lovingly reminding me that He knows my every thought and action. I felt so securely blessed and at peace. Another successful surgery!

I'd like to share one last answered prayer that happened recently. My friend's bird flew away after the cage got knocked over on the back porch. This was a special bird. It was a pretty green parakeet that had been the family pet for years. My friend's dad even taught the bird to talk. Her parents were so sad that it had flown away. When she told me about it, I told her not to worry, I was going to put the bird in my "prayer box." God knew where the bird was, and so I asked Him to keep it safe and direct it safely home. She was sure it was not going to come back, but I prayed with confidence to our God who knew right where it was. I was so sure God would take care of it for me because I asked in His name and believed it was His will. I even told my husband about it that night, and he defiantly said that it would not come home. His friend had a bird that flew away and never came back. I told him I knew it was going to come back because I asked God and believed that He would see to it's safe arrival home. The next morning, I wasn't at all surprised when my friend told me the bird had been returned by a Good Samaritan who had found the exhausted bird sitting along the side of the street. He picked the bird up, took it home, bought it some food, and placed it in an unused birdcage to keep it safe from his cats. He even posted signs in the neighborhood. Another women saw the signs, and saw the empty cage on my friend's back porch. She told my friend's father about the signs and the bird was soon returned safely home.

I could provide countless examples of answered prayer because the Lord has answered my prayers every day in ways better than I could ever asked or imagined for myself. He has shown me over the years that He will always provide for true needs, whatever we ask in His Name. We simply need to believe that He hears, and trust in His will.

The Lord desires us to seek Him and delight in Him. Psalm 37:4 reminds us to *"Delight yourself in the LORD and he will give you the desires of your heart."*

I know He does, for He has blessed me abundantly with all my heart's desires.

"*Do you not know? Have you not heard? The LORD is the everlasting God, the Creator of the ends of the earth. He will not grow tired or weary, and his understanding no one can fathom. He gives strength to the weary and increases the power of the weak.*"

Isaiah 40:28–29

9

Why Pray?

It pleases God when we pray, and He wants us to pray. As Isaiah the prophet illustrates in this scripture, God is our creator and He never grows weary and He understands more than we can ever comprehend.

When we experience the love of our Creator, only He can fill that unexplainable void in our lives with His peace and comfort.

Communion with God completes us. It makes us one with our Creator. God blesses us abundantly when we pray. He enriches our lives. It is a gift that we give to God and He gives us more than we could ever ask or imagine. It helps us to establish and strengthen our faith.

Paul stated in his letter to the Hebrews (chapter 11, verse 6):

> *"And without faith it is impossible to please God, because anyone who comes to him must believe that he exists and that he rewards those who earnestly seek him."*

Prayer is a link between this life and the next. Recently, I had a friend who died of cancer. I visited her almost weekly before she died. She loved me to bring her communion and pray with her. Her family told me at her funeral how much those visits meant to her. On the night before she died, she was heavily medicated and unable to communicate in words, only moans. When I approached her bedside she stirred a little. I spoke to her and asked her if she wanted me to prayer. Her sister nodded affirmatively that it was okay if I did. I laid my hand on her arm and stroked it gently as I began to pray. I asked that God would surround her with His love, that our Lord would hold her gently in His arms and allow her to have the most beautiful visions of heaven. I prayed for His peace and comfort upon her. As I spoke, my dear friend agreed with soft uh-huh's distinguishably different from her previous moaning. I know that if I had closed my eyes tight enough I would have seen Jesus holding her in His loving arms. I sensed His presence so strongly. It was only hours later that she passed away.

My mother died on Christmas Day at 12:25, only ten minutes after my brother and sister and I arrived. When we got there, she was breathing heavily from pneumonia. We surrounded her bed and sang "Silent Night." We prayed "The Lord's Prayer" and then we told her to go and be with the Lord, that she had suffered enough. It was so beautiful a passing we were blessed to witness. Though we had just watched our mother die, we again sensed that peace that surpasses all understanding and we felt an inexpressible Christmas joy knowing that God called our beloved mother home on the day of His birth. The night before I had written in my prayer journal that God would bless Mom with peace, love and Christmas joy, and I know she received all three that very day surrounded by her children as she entered her eternal reward.

Having been at my mother's side during her passing, and having been with my friend the night before she died, I have stood at the gates of this life and eternity and it is only a breath away. In the book of Revelation, chapter 8, verses 3 and 4, we read:

"Another angel, who had a golden censer, came and stood at the altar. He was given much incense to offer, with the prayers of all the saints, on the golden altar before the throne. The smoke of the incense, together with the prayers of the saints, went up before God from the angel's hand."

Close your eyes for a moment and contemplate the great communion of saints and angels that are gathered in the great throne room of God. They offer praise and worship to Him just as we do.

As I was attending a church service shortly after my mom's death, I honestly sensed that the heaven's opened and I could feel my mother worshiping God in the great throne room at the same time I was worshiping Him here on this earth. It was a powerful feeling, and I was sure the gates of Heaven were open and we worshipped and prayed together.

The letter of James Chapter 5 verses 13 through 16 sums it up best and gives sufficient justification as to why we should pray:

"Is any one of you in trouble? He should pray. Is anyone happy? Let him sing songs of praise. Is any one of you sick? He should call the elders of the church to pray over him and anoint him with oil in the name of the Lord. And the prayer offered in faith will make the sick person well; the Lord will raise him up. If he has sinned, he will be forgiven. Therefore confess your sins to each other and pray for each other so that you may be healed. The prayer of a righteous man is powerful and effective."

"Each time, before you intercede, be quiet first, and worship God in His glory. Think of what He can do, and how He delights to hear the prayers of His redeemed people. Think of your place and privilege in Christ, and expect great things!"

—Andrew Murray

10

Your Prayers

The rest of this book is meant for your prayers. Remember to offer them lovingly to God as a gift. Place them in His hands with confidence, knowing that He hears every word you utter.

Center on Him, focus on Him, He is the one who listens and loves you more than you could ever imagine. And if you don't know what to write, ask the Holy Spirit for His wisdom. He will intercede for you.

Remember He desires you to seek Him, whatever time you have to spend with the Lord. Perhaps you are suffering from an ailment or an illness. Perhaps you are unemployed. Whatever your circumstances, God knows it all. He waits for you to call upon Him. He wants you to look to Him for His peace, comfort, strength and wisdom. If you are experiencing a "time out" in your life because of situations beyond your control, then perhaps God has called you to this quiet time to dwell with Him and experience His perfect love. In the weeks I was recuperating from my surgery, He provided me with the respite I needed and time and enlightenment to write this book. He wants to give you rest from life's burdens. Jesus said, *"Come to me, all you who are weary and burdened, and I will give you rest. Take my yoke upon you and learn from me, for I am gentle and humble in heart, and you will find rest for your souls. For my yoke is easy and my burden is light." Matthew 11:28-30*

Call upon Him. Rest in His love. He will show you the way. He will provide all your needs. In closing, let's pray together:

Dear Heavenly Father,

Thank you for the precious gift of prayer! You are the God of love and mercy. Holy and mighty is Your name. We worship and adore You. You are the Potter, we are the clay. Mold us into perfection as You teach us to use the talents You have bestowed upon us. We place our trust in You.

We come before You with sincere hearts to honor and extol You above all, Dear Lord, Jesus Christ, our Redeemer and friend.

We humble ourselves before you for we are sinful. Have mercy on us and forgive us for all the wrongs we have done.

Guide and direct us in all we do. Grant us Your grace and wisdom to lead lives that will glorify You. Teach us to be kind and loving.

We thank you for reading our hearts and knowing what is on our mind. We entrust to You all those we love and all those who most need our prayers.

For all the children in this world, Lord. May they be loved and cared for and may they always feel Your love. Dear Father, we live in a world with many dangers and problems. Keep us safe from harm, and heal our nation's ills.

You know the needs of the church. Rid it of corruption, and unite us as one body of believers so one day we might worship together in Your Most Precious Name.

Thank you for all the gifts You bestow on us, and for your life-sustaining words. They are the words of everlasting life. We are grateful for all the blessings we receive each day from Your loving hands.

May our prayers always be pleasing to You, Father, We love you Lord.

As we present our needs to You,
Let us wrap them in a gift box of praise and
Line it with tissue paper of thanksgiving and trust.
Enfold it with magnificent wrappings of adoration,
Lovingly tape it with confidence,
Unselfishly tie it with ribbons of hope,
Instantly cut the strands of doubt and anxiety, and
Adoringly offer our Gift to you, Oh God, lovingly and entirely.

Alleluia!

In Jesus Most Precious Name,

Amen!

GWH	CAO	EJO
BAQ	DEQ	LMo
AMF	TLM	CBK
TAF	JLS	RJP

Journal Pages

_____
_____
_____
_____
_____
_____
_____
_____
_____
_____
_____
_____
_____
_____
_____
_____
_____
_____
_____
_____

*Your word is a lamp to my feet
and a light for my path.*

Psalm 119:105

_____
_____
_____
_____
_____
_____
_____
_____
_____
_____
_____
_____
_____
_____
_____
_____
_____
_____
_____
_____

*I can do everything through
Christ who gives me strength.*

Philippians 4:13

_____
_____
_____
_____
_____
_____
_____
_____
_____
_____
_____
_____
_____
_____
_____
_____
_____
_____
_____
_____
_____
_____
_____

And we know that in all things God works for the good of those who love him, who have been called according to his purpose.

Romans 8:28

_____

_____

_____

_____

_____

_____

_____

_____

_____

_____

_____

_____

_____

_____

_____

_____

_____

_____

_____

_____

_____

_____

Come to me, all you who are weary and burdened, and I will give you rest.

Matthew 11:28

_____
_____
_____
_____
_____
_____
_____
_____
_____
_____
_____
_____
_____
_____
_____
_____
_____
_____
_____
_____

Delight yourself in the LORD and he will give you the desires of your heart.

Psalm 37:4

_____
_____
_____
_____
_____
_____
_____
_____
_____
_____
_____
_____
_____
_____
_____
_____
_____
_____
_____
_____
_____
_____
_____

Trust in the LORD with all your heart and lean not on your own understanding; in all your ways acknowledge him and he will make your paths straight.

Proverbs 3:5-6

_____

_____

_____

_____

_____

_____

_____

_____

_____

_____

_____

_____

_____

_____

_____

_____

_____

_____

_____

_____

_____

_____

Yet, O LORD, you are our Father. We are the clay, you are the potter; we are all the work of your hand.

Isaiah 64:8

_____
_____
_____
_____
_____
_____
_____
_____
_____
_____
_____
_____
_____
_____
_____
_____
_____
_____
_____

Therefore I tell you, do not worry about your life, what you will eat; or about your body, what you will wear. Life is more than food, and the body more than clothes. But seek his kingdom, and these things will be given to you as well.

Luke 12:22-23,31

_____
_____
_____
_____
_____
_____
_____
_____
_____
_____
_____
_____
_____
_____
_____
_____
_____
_____
_____
_____

"Because he loves me," says the LORD, "I will rescue him; I will protect him, for he acknowledges my name. He will call upon me, and I will answer him; I will be with him in trouble, . . .

Psalm 91:14-15a

_____

_____

_____

_____

_____

_____

_____

_____

_____

_____

_____

_____

_____

_____

_____

_____

_____

_____

Do not be anxious about anything, but in everything, by prayer and petition, with thanksgiving, present your requests to God. And the peace of God, which transcends all understanding, will guard your hearts and your minds in Christ Jesus.

Philippians 4:6-7

_____
_____
_____
_____
_____
_____
_____
_____
_____
_____
_____
_____
_____
_____
_____
_____
_____
_____
_____
_____
_____

"Therefore I tell you, whatever you ask for in prayer, believe that you have received it, and it will be yours. And when you stand praying, if you hold anything against anyone, forgive him, so that your Father in heaven may forgive you your sins."

Mark 11:22-25

_____

_____

_____

_____

_____

_____

_____

_____

_____

_____

_____

_____

_____

_____

_____

_____

_____

_____

_____

_____

_____

_____

"With man this is impossible, but with God all things are possible."

Matthew 19:26

_____
_____
_____
_____
_____
_____
_____
_____
_____
_____
_____
_____
_____
_____
_____
_____
_____
_____
_____
_____
_____

*The LORD is righteous in all his
ways and loving toward all he
has made.
The LORD is near to all who
call on him, to all who call on
him in truth. He fulfills the
desires of those who fear him; he
hears their cry and saves them.*

Psalm 145:17-19

_____

_____

_____

_____

_____

_____

_____

_____

_____

_____

_____

_____

_____

_____

_____

_____

_____

_____

_____

_____

_____

_____

_____

"…I tell you the truth, if you have faith as small as a mustard seed, you can say to this mountain, 'Move from here to there' and it will move. Nothing will be impossible for you."

Matthew 17:20

_____
_____
_____
_____
_____
_____
_____
_____
_____
_____
_____
_____
_____
_____
_____
_____
_____
_____
_____

"This is the confidence we have in approaching God: that if we ask anything according to his will, he hears us."

1 John 5:14

"And pray in the Spirit on all occasions with all kinds of prayers and requests. With this in mind, be alert and always keep on praying for all the saints. "

Ephesians 6:18

_____
_____
_____
_____
_____
_____
_____
_____
_____
_____
_____
_____
_____
_____
_____
_____
_____
_____
_____
_____
_____
_____
_____

Therefore confess your sins to each other and pray for each other so that you may be healed. The prayer of a righteous man is powerful and effective.

James 5:16

_____

_____

_____

_____

_____

_____

_____

_____

_____

_____

_____

_____

_____

_____

_____

_____

_____

_____

_____

_____

_____

*"Do not let your hearts be
troubled. Trust in God; trust also
in me. In my Father's house are
many rooms; if it were not so, I
would have told you. I am going
there to prepare a place for you."*

John 14:1-3

_____

_____

_____

_____

_____

_____

_____

_____

_____

_____

_____

_____

_____

_____

_____

_____

_____

_____

_____

_____

_____

_____

Jesus answered, "I am the way and the truth and the life. No one comes to the Father except through me."

John 14:6

_____
_____
_____
_____
_____
_____
_____
_____
_____
_____
_____
_____
_____
_____
_____
_____
_____
_____
_____
_____
_____
_____

"Now to him who is able to do immeasurably more than all we ask or imagine, according to his power that is at work within us, to him be glory in the church and in Christ Jesus throughout all generations, for ever and ever! Amen."

Ephesians 3:20-21

_____

_____

_____

_____

_____

_____

_____

_____

_____

_____

_____

_____

_____

_____

_____

_____

_____

_____

_____

"Do you not know? Have you not heard? The LORD is the everlasting God, the Creator of the ends of the earth. He will not grow tired or weary, and his understanding no one can fathom. He gives strength to the weary and increases the power of the weak."

Isaiah 40:28–29

_____

_____

_____

_____

_____

_____

_____

_____

_____

_____

_____

_____

_____

_____

_____

_____

_____

_____

_____

_____

*And without faith it is impossible
to please God, because anyone who
comes to him must believe that he
exists and that he rewards those
who earnestly seek him.*

Hebrews 11:6

_____

_____

_____

_____

_____

_____

_____

_____

_____

_____

_____

_____

_____

_____

_____

_____

_____

If any of you lacks wisdom, he should ask God, who gives generously to all without finding fault, and it will be given to him. But when he asks, he must believe and not doubt, because he who doubts is like a wave of the sea, blown and tossed by the wind. That man should not think he will receive anything from the Lord;

James 1:5-7

_____
_____
_____
_____
_____
_____
_____
_____
_____
_____
_____
_____
_____
_____
_____
_____
_____
_____
_____
_____
_____
_____

*Every good and perfect gift is
from above, coming down from
the Father of the heavenly lights,
who does not change like shifting
shadows.*

James 1:17

_____

_____

_____

_____

_____

_____

_____

_____

_____

_____

_____

_____

_____

_____

_____

_____

_____

_____

_____

_____

_____

*Command those who are rich in
this present world not to be arro-
gant nor to put their hope in
wealth, which is so uncertain,
but to put their hope in God, who
richly provides us with everything
for our enjoyment.*

1 Timothy 6:17

_____
_____
_____
_____
_____
_____
_____
_____
_____
_____
_____
_____
_____
_____
_____
_____
_____
_____
_____
_____
_____
_____

*For God so loved the world that
he gave his one and only Son,
that whoever believes in him shall
not perish but have eternal life.*

John 3:16

Scriptural References by Chapter

Gift of Prayer

Scripture	The Verse or Content
Psalm 141:2	Our prayers come like incense before God
1 John 3:22-23	We receive what we ask
Phillipians 4:6	Don't be anxious about anything

Childhood Prayers

Revelation 21:10-11	John was shown the holy city
Revelation 21:18-21	Description of the heavenly city

God's Word on Prayer

Romans 8:26-28	In the same way the spirit helps us…
Matthew 6:8-15	Our Father, who art in heaven…
John 11:41b-42	Father, I thank you that you have heard me
Matthew 7:7-8,11b	Ask and it will be given to you;
Matthew 17:20	I tell you the truth, if you have faith as small
Matthew 18:19-20	Again I tell you, that if two of you…
Luke 18:1	Pray always and not lose hope
John 14:14	Ask anything in His name…
John 15:7	Abide in Him and what we ask will be done.
1 John 5:14	This is the confidence we have…
Ephesians 6:18	And pray in the Spirit on all occassions…
1 Timothy 2:1-6	I urge then, first of all, that requests, prayers
James 5:16-18	The prayer of a righteous man is powerful…
Sirach 7:10	Don't be impatient in our prayers.
Sirach 35:16-18	He who serves God willingly is heard...

Intercessory Prayer

1 Timothy 2:1-6	I urge then, first of all, that requests, prayers
Ephesians 6:18	Pray for each other every chance we get.

| Phillipians 4:6-7 | Do not be anxious about anything |
| Matthew 5:44-45 | Love your enemies and pray for those |

Family Prayer

Matthew 18:19-20	Again I tell you, that if two of you...
1 Peter 3:12	For the eyes of the Lord are on the righteous
James 5:16	...The prayer of a righteous man is powerful

Walking with God in Prayer

Micah 6:8	He has showed you oh man what is good.
Proverbs 3:5-6	Trust in the Lord with all your heart.
1 Corinthians 11:23-26	The Lord Jesus on the night He was betrayed

My Prayer Chair

Mark 1:35	Very early in the morning while it was still
1 Samuel 3	The Lord called to Samuel...
1 Kings 19	Go out and stand on the mountain...
John 14:1-4, 6	Don't let your hearts be troubled...
Matthew 4:19	Come follow me...

Answered Prayers and Blessings

Psalm 91	He who dwells in the shelter of the most High
Ephesians 3:20-21	Now to Him who is able to do immeasurably
Psalm 139	Oh Lord you have searched me and you...
Psalm 37:4	Delight yourself in the Lord

Why Pray?

Isaiah 40:28-29	Do you not know, have you not heard
Hebrews 11:6	And without faith it is impossible to please
Revelations 8:3-4	Another angel who had a golden censer...
James 5:13-16	Is anyone of you in trouble? He should pray...

Your Prayers

| Matthew 11:28-30 | Come to me all you who are weary... |